spot

SPORTS

TRACK AND FIELD

by Mari Schuh

AMICUS | AMICUS INK

shot

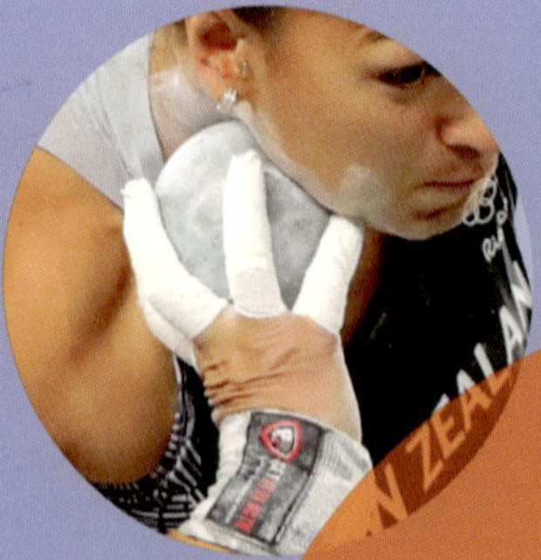

bar

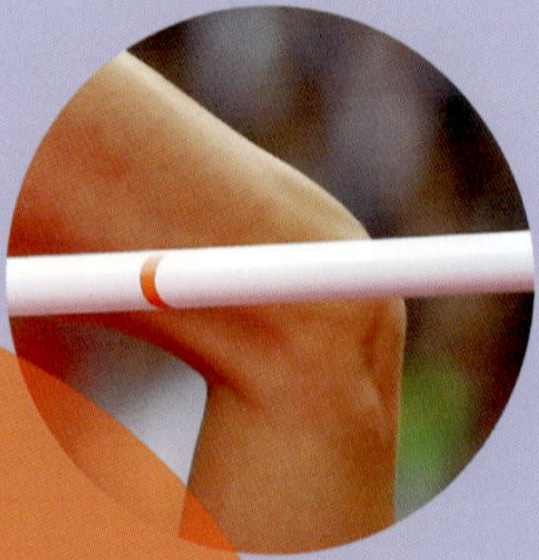

Look for these words and pictures as you read.

lane

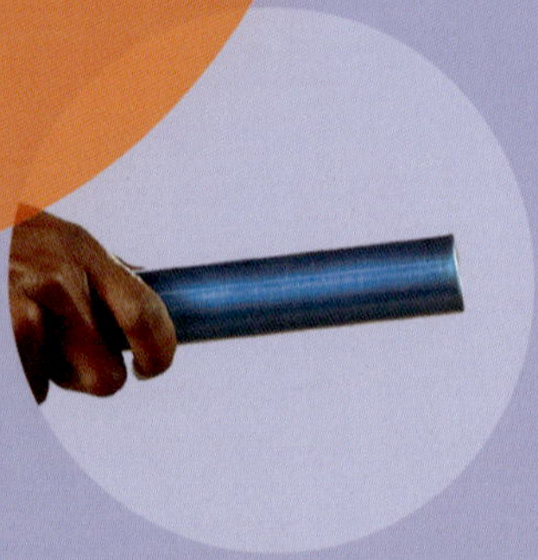

baton

Let's watch the track meet!

The runners take their marks.

Get set. Go!

Ten teams are at today's meet.
Runners race on the big track.
Other events are on the field.

Rio2016

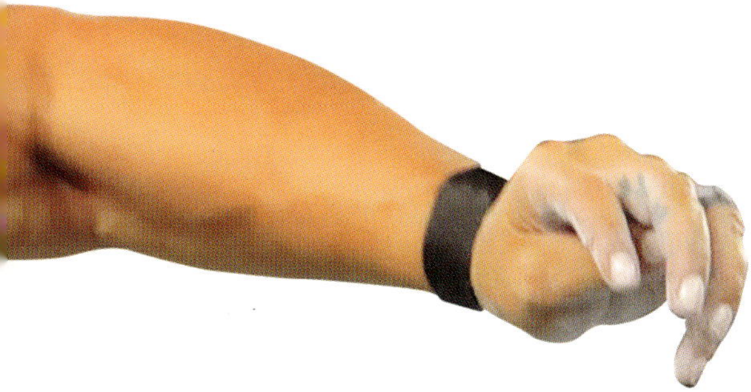

shot

Do you see the shot?
It is a heavy ball.
She spins. She throws.

bar

Do you see the bar?
She leaps over it.
She wins the high jump!

Do you see the lane?
This track has nine lanes.

lane

2

Do you see the baton? A runner passes it. Four runners make one relay team.

baton

The runners cross the finish line. Wow! The race is close!

shot

bar

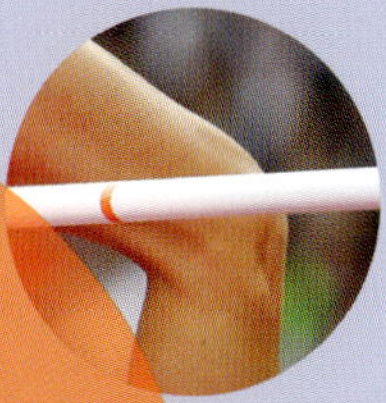

Did you find?

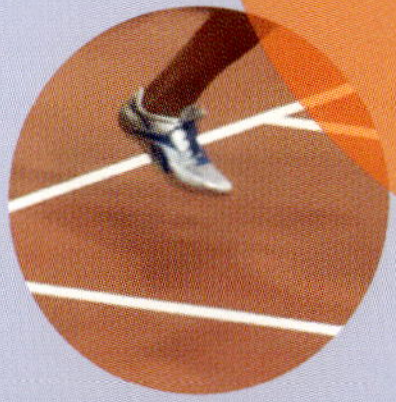

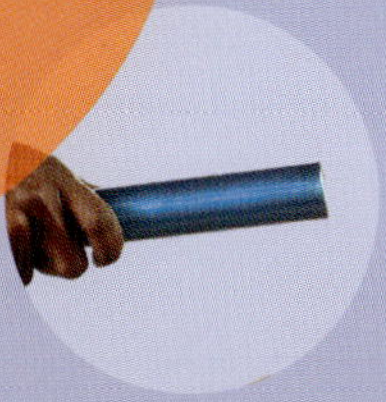

lane

baton

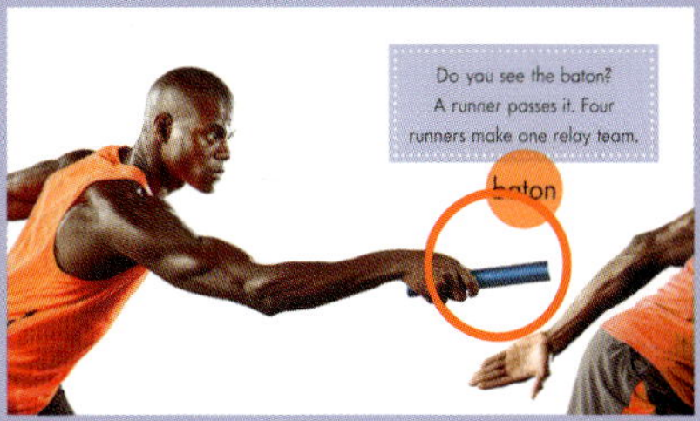

spot

Spot is published by Amicus and Amicus Ink
P.O. Box 1329, Mankato, MN 56002
www.amicuspublishing.us

Library of Congress Cataloging-in-Publication Data
Names: Schuh, Mari C., 1975- author. | Schuh, Mari C., 1975- Sports. | Amicus (Firm)
Title: Track & field / Mari C. Schuh.
Other titles: Track and field
Description: Mankato, Minnesota : Amicus, 2021. | Series: Spot. Sports | Audience: Ages 4-7 | Audience: Grades K-1 |
Summary: "Elementary sports fans will clear key vocabulary hurdles in this high-interest leveled reader about track and field events. Simple text and color photos touch on the shot put, high jump, and running events. A search-and-find feature reinforces key vocabulary"-- Provided by publisher.
Identifiers: LCCN 2019036341 (print) | LCCN 2019036342 (ebook) | ISBN 9781681519401 (Library Binding) | ISBN 9781681525877 (Paperback) | ISBN 9781645490258 (PDF)
Subjects: LCSH: Track and field--Juvenile literature. | Illustrated children's books. | Readers.
Classification: LCC GV1060.55 .S36 2021 (print) | LCC GV1060.55 (ebook) | DDC 796.42--dc23
LC record available at https://lccn.loc.gov/2019036341
LC ebook record available at https://lccn.loc.gov/2019036342

Printed in the United States of America

HC 10 9 8 7 6 5 4 3 2 1
PB 10 9 8 7 6 5 4 3 2 1

For Coach Bob Bonk and the
Fairmont Cardinals —MS

Gillia Olson, editor
Deb Miner, series designer
Aubrey Harper, book designer
and photo researcher

Photos by AP/David J. Phillip 14–15, Lee Jin-man 3, Matt Dunham 8–9, Michael Kappeler 6–7; Getty/City-Press 4–5; iStock/4x6 1, anton5146 cover, 16, Moof 12–13; Newscom/Eleanor Scriven/robertharding 10–11